Bobby Clarke

Bobby Clarke

EDWARD F. DOLAN, JR.
and RICHARD B. LYTTLE

Doubleday & Company, Inc.
Garden City, New York

Library of Congress Cataloging in Publication Data
Dolan, Edward F   1924–
    Bobby Clarke.
    SUMMARY: A biography of the hockey player who was
twice voted Most Valuable Player in the National Hockey
League.
    1. Clarke, Bobby, 1949–   —Juvenile literature.
2. Hockey players—Canada—Biography—Juvenile
literature.   3. Philadelphia Flyers (Hockey club)—
Juvenile literature. [1. Clarke, Bobby, 1949–
2. Hockey players] I. Lyttle, Richard B., joint
author. II. Title.
GV848.5.C58D64   796.9′62′0924 [B] [920]
ISBN 0-385-12523-2
Library of Congress Catalog Card Number 76–56280

This book is for Mark Dolan

Contents

1

Player and Leader

The puck flew into the corner and banged off the boards. The two skaters raced for it.

The big man in the blue-and-white uniform reached the corner first. He tried to get his stick on the puck. But it was no use. His stick was knocked aside as his opponent, a smaller man wearing an orange-and-black jersey, came flying in.

Ker-thump! A shoulder drove the big man against the wall. One of his gloves came off and flipped over the rail. The roar of the crowd shook the arena.

The big man fought for his breath. He was being held against the rail by the smaller man's knees and shoulders. He saw the puck between his skates and the boards. But he couldn't go for it. He was off balance and locked against the wall.

The referee's whistle shrilled.

Face-off.

The crowd roared again. Some of the fans began clapping as Bobby Clarke released the big man and skated easily away. There was a gap-toothed grin on Bobby's impish face. He glanced at his teammates as he glided to the face-off circle.

Now the clapping turned to a rhythmic beat. The grin widened to a smile, and the fans cheered. They loved that toothless smile. They loved everything about Bobby Clarke, and everything that he did.

He wore No. 16 on the back of his jersey. On the front, above his heart, there was a block C. The C really wasn't needed. Every player on the ice and every one of the 15,000 hometown fans in the arena knew that Bobby Clarke was captain of the Philadelphia Flyers.

You could tell it from his confidence. From the way he skated and handled himself. From the energy and spirit that he put into every play. And from the look he had just given his teammates. It seemed to say:

"Okay, you guys. I'm doing my job. You do yours."

Bobby was indeed doing his job. By forcing the face-off deep in the enemy zone, he had set up a good chance for a Flyer goal—a goal that could beat the New York Rangers in these final seconds of play. It was a typical Flyer move. Face-offs were good for Philadelphia because Bobby usually won them.

Now he and the Ranger moved into the face-off circle. They tensed. They waited, sticks ready. The puck dropped between them. Their sticks blurred. Wood crashed against wood.

Suddenly, Bobby spun away, his stick on the puck. He passed hard to his point man. Bang! The point man slapped a shot at the Ranger goal. The goalie lunged. He blocked the shot as he fell, but the puck bounced loose. Reggie Leach, one of Bobby's linemates, was there. He flipped the puck over the fallen goalie for the game's winning score.

Leach, holding his arms and stick aloft, skated to Bobby. The two men crashed happily into each other in a bear hug. The roar of the fans was like thunder.

Leach, of course, was credited for the winning goal. Bobby had set it up, but under hockey's scoring system, he was not even given an assist on the official scorer's card. But that didn't cut down one bit on his big grin when he bearhugged Leach.

"That's Bobby for you," a teammate says. "He doesn't care who scores the points. He just cares about helping the Flyers to win. He's a completely unselfish guy."

Bobby Clarke has been helping the Flyers win games since 1969. Along the way, he's become one of the great centers in the National Hockey League, a man famous for his all-around play. Sportswriters say he's not as flashy as Bobby Hull or Gordie Howe, but they agree that he's about as solid a player as you'll ever find.

Just look at his skills. He can check. He can pass. He can shoot. He can run power plays. He can kill penalties. And he can win face-offs. The Flyers were a losing team when he joined them. No one will argue with any Philadelphia fan who says that Bobby did much to turn them into the winners they are today.

To help his team win, Bobby has always played hard. He

13

is known as one of the toughest, most aggressive men in the league. He has to be. Hockey's a rough game. But it's gotten rougher than ever in the past fifteen years and is now marked by much violence and fighting. Bobby doesn't think the violence is good for the game. But you can't let the enemy walk all over you.

And, to help his team win, he has become one of the most respected captains in the league. He works with players who are in a slump. He's quick to bawl out anyone who lets down. He's just as quick to slap a teammate on the back for a good play.

And, above all, Bobby looks on himself not as a star or a captain but as a team player. He's won more hockey awards than any other Flyer. But he says they're really team awards. He won't take them home. They stay in the Philadelphia clubhouse.

Off the ice, he supplies the same kind of leadership. He works with the coach in developing game plans. He helps the Flyers to make player trades. Then he meets new players at the airport and puts them up at his house until they can find a place to live.

The fans in other cities don't like his rough play and his winning ways, but his teammates know him as a modest, generous man. As one friend says, he doesn't strut around like a "big hockey star." His favorite everyday outfit is a golf shirt, Levi's, and a pair of milk-stained clogs. Each summer, he takes the team's trainers and their wives to Florida for a vacation at his expense. He runs a preseason training camp for young players.

Star player and team leader—that's Bobby Clarke. How did he get where he is today?

It's a story of hard work. And the story of being determined to play hockey even when you have an incurable illness.

It's a story that begins in a small town in the province of Manitoba, Canada—a town with the strange name of Flin Flon.

2

A Big Ambition

Back in 1915, a man named Tom Creighton was prospecting for gold in the wilds of northern Canada. One day, while crossing a frozen lake with four friends, he fell through the thin ice. His friends fished him out, helped him to a cave, and built a fire. As he warmed himself, he saw that the heat from the fire was melting the ice and snow on the cave walls.

His eyes widened. Something was glittering beneath the whiteness. It looked like—gold! He forgot that he was soaking wet. He and his friends quickly dug into the walls. Sure enough, it was gold. Plenty of it. And the ores of copper, zinc, and silver as well.

Creighton was amazed. This was something that could only happen in a book. Suddenly he remembered a story he had once read. Called *The Sunless City*, it had been about the fantastic adventures of a Professor Josiah Flintabbatey Flonatin, who explored a bottomless lake in a submarine and came upon a city of gold.

Creighton laughed and decided to name his discovery after the professor. The name was soon shortened to Flin Flon.

Today, Creighton's mine is one of the richest in all Canada. It is carved into solid rock and is five thousand feet deep. On top of it sits the town of Flin Flon.

Flin Flon is a comfortable town of twelve thousand people. Most of the men there work in the mine. One of the miners is Cliff Clarke, Bobby's father.

Cliff Clarke first came to Flin Flon in 1941, when he was sixteen. He planned just a short visit with his uncle, but he liked the town and decided to stay. He worked for a while in a hardware store and then took a job in the mine. He became a driller, the key man in a dynamite crew. Later on, he met and married a young woman named Yvonne.

Bobby was their first child. He was born on August 13, 1949. His full name is Robert Earle Clarke.

Like so many children in Canada, Bobby was raised in a town that loves hockey. In fact, hockey is almost as important as mining in Flin Flon. Everyone talks about it. Everyone follows the amateur and professional leagues. Practically every boy and a good many girls play the game. They start early, some of them as soon as they can stand on a pair of skates.

Flin Flon is an ideal place for hockey. The Arctic Circle is less than a thousand miles away, and so the winters are always long and cold. The lakes and rivers around the town are frozen over for months each year. And when the ice melts, the youngsters take their skates and sticks to the local rink and go right on practicing and playing.

Bobby put on his first pair of skates when he was four years old. Right then, his whole future was settled. He loved to skate. He wanted to be on the ice all the time. His home overlooked a river, and he was always to be found down there in the winter months. The temperature might drop to forty below zero, but that didn't bother him.

Nothing about skating bothered him—not the cold, not his numb toes, not the long hours of practice, not the bruises and the falls. As young as he was, he was fired with a great ambition: He was going to become a top hockey player one day.

Soon after he started school, Bobby made an unhappy discovery. Classes interfered with hockey. In fact, if you let it, school could take away practically all of your ice time. Bobby decided not to let this happen.

Sometimes, after telling his mother he was going to school, he would sneak down to the river instead. And there were times when he didn't have to lie. He and his close friend John Rutley learned that the teachers would send you home if you misbehaved in class. Bobby and John would pull some stunt and then head for the river.

Many times, Yvonne Clarke would look out her window and think that one of the boys on the river looked like Bobby. She'd tell herself that it couldn't be, but then, sure enough, the telephone would ring. A teacher would be on the line, saying that Bobby had been sent home for making trouble.

The river was fine, but Bobby wanted a rink right at home. So he flooded the backyard whenever the temperature dropped below freezing. Then the whack of the puck against the house became a common sound for the Clarke family. It sometimes woke his baby sister Roxanne. Once there was the sound of glass shattering as a badly aimed puck flew through a window.

Though his home "rink" was handy, it was big enough for practice only. To find a game, Bobby had to go to a park where boys and girls of his age gathered. The kids were always choosing up sides, but Bobby didn't think the games were much fun. There were no supervisors to help you correct your mistakes and skate better. Bobby wanted to be on a regular team. He wanted a uniform. He wanted a coach.

In all, he wanted to get into league play.

League hockey for young people is played throughout Canada. There are leagues for players of all ages. The highest of the leagues is for Juniors, young men seventeen years and older. Many great professional stars come from the Junior ranks.

For Bobby, there was one great problem. In Flin Flon, the youngest children played in the Tom Thumb League. You had to be nine years old before you could sign up for it. Bobby had a long wait ahead of him.

It was tough to wait. It became very tough in 1957, when Flin Flon's Junior team, the Bombers, took the Canadian Junior Championship by beating the Hull-Ottawa Canadiens. It was the biggest thing that happened in town since old Tom Creighton fell through the ice.

Now Bobby knew he had to get into league hockey right away. He would be eight in August, still a year too young. But he noticed that the Tom Thumb coaches didn't check the birth certificates too often when players signed up. You just might be able to lie about your age and get away with it.

That's just what Bobby did. He began playing for a Tom Thumb team called the Westleys when he was eight years old. The team was coached by Earl Garinger.

It seems that Bobby didn't make much of an impression on his coach. The boy was thin and so nearsighted that he had to wear glasses when he skated. He was also shy, much quieter than other boys and girls his age. Garinger watched him on the ice and rated him as just an average skater.

Two things, however, did catch Garinger's attention. First, like so many beginners on ice, Bobby had ankle problems. But they were a special sort. Most young ankles bend in. Bobby's bent out.

Second, the boy did have one great quality, his attitude. He wanted to be the best player possible. He always listened closely to what Garinger said. There was no horseplay with Bobby. He gave himself 100 per cent to the game.

Garinger's team practiced on a small outdoor rink behind his house. It was there that Bobby got his first real lessons at stick-handling. The little rink was almost always jammed with boys and girls. It was a challenge to move the puck through such a crowd. The determined Bobby worked hard at learning to do so. At the end of Bobby's first season, Garinger admitted that the boy was greatly improved in stick-handling.

But still the coach didn't think much of Bobby's abilities. Three years later, after Bobby had played for other youth teams, Garinger again pegged him as an average skater. He just couldn't see any potential for the future in the boy.

Bobby, however, held onto his ambition. He would be a professional one day. He would play in the National Hockey League. He was sure of it.

Nothing could stop him—not even serious illness.

(Photo: Clifton Boutelle)

Bobby wears an impish grin when he moves in for a face-off. The chances are good that he will win possession for the Flyers. *(Photo: Clifton Boutelle)*

Checked against the boards, Inge Hammarstrom of the Toronto Maple Leafs can do nothing to reach the puck. The action is typical of Bobby Clarke's hard play. *(Photo: United Press International)*

Bobby holds his position solidly between the puck and his opponent as he looks for a pass. *(Photo: Clifton Boutelle)*

In perfect scoring position, Bobby takes a whack from a defender's stick as he tries to locate the puck during action against the Detroit Red Wings. *(Photo: Clifton Boutelle)*

Flin Flon, Manitoba, has plenty of water for natural ice. This shot, looking east across Ross Lake, was taken just after an October snow, about a month before freeze-up. *(Photo: Ron Dobson)*

Youngsters can play hockey all year long inside Flin Flon's Whitney Forum. The ten-year-old on the left wears Bobby Clarke's number. *(Photo: Ron Dobson)*

In honor of the fictional character who gave the town its name, Flin Flon residents had cartoonist Al Capp design this statue of Josiah Flintabbatey Flonatin. *(Photo: Ron Dobson)*

Reminders of Bobby are everywhere in Flin Flon. Here a No. 16 jersey stands out in the Bombers' dressing room. *(Photo: Ron Dobson)*

Bobby ducks away from Bert Marshall's glove during action against the New York Islanders. (*Photo: United Press International*)

A good talker keeps his team together. Here Bobby skates into the open, yelling for a teammate's pass. (*Photo: Clifton Boutelle*)

Bobby fakes out a defender . . .
(Photo: Clifton Boutelle)

gets the puck . . . *(Photo: Clifton Boutelle)*

and closes for a shot on goal. *(Photo: Clifton Boutelle)*

3

Diabetes and Hockey

Bobby Clarke was fifteen years old when he learned that he had diabetes. The doctors who discovered his case told him that he would have to give up hockey.

Diabetes is an incurable disease. No one knows what causes it. Those who have it cannot change sugar and starches into body energy because of a shortage of a chemical called insulin. Before scientists learned how to make insulin in the laboratory, most people who had diabetes died while they were still very young.

Now, however, with special diets and daily injections of insulin, most diabetics can lead normal lives. But athletes do not lead normal lives. Playing as hard as they do, they need far more body energy than the average person.

Bobby's doctors said that he might be able to play the goaltender spot but that he could never skate all over the rink in a game and still keep his health. Cliff and Yvonne Clarke believed the doctors at first. Bobby didn't. With insulin injections and a special diet, he felt great. So why not go on playing? Why not go on planning to be a pro? Those questions set all his friends to shaking their heads.

For Bobby, this was the toughest thing about diabetes. People were prejudiced against it. They were afraid of it. Sure, they said, you feel fine now. But sooner or later, it will leave you too weak and tired for play. And it's incurable.

Fortunately, there were some doctors who kept an open mind about Bobby's case. They told his parents that the controls for diabetes seemed to work best when the patient got plenty of exercise. If Bobby took care of himself, the doctors said, he might be able to play hockey.

This was enough for Bobby, but his parents were not so sure. In December of 1964, Cliff Clarke took Bobby to Winnipeg to see a specialist.

A trip to the city was a big event for a Flin Flon boy. Cliff Clarke thought that Bobby would be impressed with the city lights, particularly the Christmas lights in the stores. If nothing else, his father told himself, the trip would take Bobby's mind off hockey.

It didn't work out that way. As soon as they arrived, Bobby grabbed his skates and went looking for a hockey rink. He found one on the outskirts of the city. He sat there the whole evening and watched some youngsters play.

The next day, after giving Bobby a series of tests, the Winnipeg specialist had some good news. He said that

Bobby could go on playing. The doctor told him that base-
ball players Ron Santo and Bill Nicholson, tennis star Billy
Talbert, and several other great athletes were all diabetics.
Bobby didn't have to let the disease stand in the way of his
ambition. But the doctor warned him to stick to his diet
and never miss a daily injection of insulin. If he didn't do
this, his body would fail him.

The doctor's report was actually more important to his
parents than it was to Bobby himself. He had already decided to go on playing no matter what the doctor said. But
now his parents were with him all the way.

When he turned seventeen, Bobby finally became eligi-
ble for Junior hockey. He tried out for the Flin Flon
Bombers. Like Garinger, Bomber coach Pat Ginnell was
not impressed with the young man when he first saw him.

A skinny kid with buck teeth and eyeglasses just wasn't
the coach's idea of a hockey star. Bobby had reached his
full height of five feet ten by now, but he hadn't yet filled
out. Ginnell wondered if the boy had a chance. Then he
saw him flash along the ice. Bobby had worked hard in the
years since first joining a Tom Thumb team. Ginnell knew
that this was going to be one of the best players he had
ever coached.

Bobby made the team easily. No sooner did he put on a
Bomber uniform for the first time than he dropped out of
high school.

His parents were disappointed, but not really surprised.
They knew that Bobby wanted to be a professional and
that he had always spent more time skating than studying.
And they knew that the Bombers practiced daily and

played a full schedule. Much time was spent traveling to games in distant towns and cities. Some trips lasted two days or more. There just wouldn't be time for school.

Actually, no one in Flin Flon expected Junior skaters to continue school. Junior play was considered all-important because it was the doorway to professional hockey. Today, many Junior players go on to college and do not enter the pro ranks until they earn their degrees. But when Bobby first joined the league, college meant little to the players. They wanted to get into professional hockey as soon as possible.

During his first season with the Bombers, Bobby put on weight, building toward his 180 pounds of today. The added pounds improved his performance, and Ginnell was pleased. Playing center, the boy never turned in a bad game. By his second season—1967–68—Bobby was leading the Bombers' attack.

That season, he played in 59 games, scored 51 goals, and turned in 117 assists. His point total of 168 was one of the best in all Canada. Ginnell felt sure that Bobby Clarke would one day be a big name in professional hockey. There was just one hitch: the diabetes.

When scouts from the teams in the National Hockey League came to look at the Bombers, they showed little interest in Bobby. They had heard that "the kid is sick." Sure, they were impressed with the way he played. And they especially liked his hustle and desire. All this should have made him a top prospect for the pros. But the scouts weren't ready to recommend someone with diabetes.

Their prejudice angered Ginnell. He knew that Bobby's driving ambition was to break into professional hockey.

The boy deserved the chance. He had an excellent record, and his illness had never kept him from turning in a top-notch job on the ice. Something had to be done to make the scouts change their minds.

The coach hit on a plan. Before Bobby's third and final Junior season—1968–69—Ginnell took him to the Mayo Clinic at Rochester, Minnesota. He wanted the doctors there to examine Bobby and give him a good health report, one that could be shown to the scouts.

And that's exactly what he got—a good report. The doctors said that there was no reason why Bobby could not play professional hockey. All he had to do was take good care of himself.

A happy Bobby returned to Flin Flon. He took an off-season job in a garage and sometimes drove a tow truck to earn extra money. The work kept him in good shape for the coming season. His spirits were high when league play finally began. He had the report from the clinic. Now if he could have a good season, he felt that his dream might come true.

His record for the 1968–69 season was not only good, it was excellent. As the leader of the Bombers' attack, he took a lot of pressure from the opposing teams. They felt that if they could stop the hard-driving center, they could beat the Bombers. But he wouldn't be stopped. The Flin Flon team racked up a winning season, with Bobby scoring 51 goals and 86 assists. This gave him a total of 137 points and once again put him among the top scorers in the league.

Altogether, Bobby played in 58 games that season. In addition, he began to show a talent for leadership. He seemed to spark the team in every game. Even during practice he got the best effort out of his teammates. Once, when some of the Bombers started goofing off, Bobby jumped on them before Ginnell had a chance to say a thing.

"I want to play hockey for a living," Bobby shouted. "You guys are hurting me, and you're hurting the team. So shape up!"

Usually, Bobby did not have to say a thing to keep his teammates in line. He just worked twice as hard as everyone else and set an example for all the Bombers to follow.

But all the good work didn't pay off so far as the NHL scouts were concerned. Nor did the good report from the Mayo Clinic. The scouts agreed that Bobby was a top prospect and that the doctors knew about medicine. But what did the doctors know about pro hockey? No one seemed willing to take a chance on a diabetic.

It was a bad time for both Bobby and Ginnell. They had tried their hardest. Now there was just one chance left. The NHL each year drafts Junior players. Bobby could only wait for the draft and hope that some team would think enough of him to forget his diabetes.

The draft was held in June 1969. Owners, managers, and scouts for the twelve NHL clubs gathered at the Queen Elizabeth Hotel in Montreal. They sat down to decide the fate of the best Junior players.

Bobby crossed his fingers.

4

Second Choice

Gerry Melnyk was a scout with the Philadelphia Flyers. Unlike most of the other NHL scouts, he was completely sold on Bobby. He told Bud Poile, the Flyers' general manager, that the young man was the best Junior player in all western Canada. He insisted that Bobby be the Flyers' first choice in the draft.

Poile shook his head.

He was unwilling to gamble on a diabetic, even when Melnyk told him of the Mayo Clinic report. Poile did, however, ask for the opinion of Dr. Stanley Spoont, the team physician. Dr. Spoont had never met Bobby, but he said that a player who took care of himself and followed medical advice could probably be a pro despite diabetes. In short, Dr. Spoont could find no reason not to draft Bobby.

This was enough for Poile to keep Bobby in mind, but

not as a first choice. The Flyers instead picked Robert Currier, a six-foot-six center. The other clubs also skipped over Bobby. He was still waiting when the second choices began.

But he didn't have to wait much longer.

Melnyk now had the support of Keith Allen, the Flyers' assistant general manager. Both urged Poile to take the young center on the club's next turn. Both said that if he didn't he was going to lose out on a fine player and a natural-born leader.

Poile still wasn't sure. Then he began to suspect that the Montreal Canadiens also had their eyes on the kid from Flin Flon. That did it. When the Flyers' second turn came, Poile drafted Bobby.

The decision was perhaps the best one that Poile ever made. Sixteen men were drafted ahead of Bobby. Just two of them are still playing in the NHL. Currier, the hefty center picked first by the Flyers, never became as big a star as had been hoped. Though Bobby Clarke was the seventeenth man named in the draft, there is no doubt today that he was the best of the lot.

Bobby was a little disappointed at being picked so late. It hurt. It showed that too many clubs had made up their minds about him without checking the medical facts. But he soon forgot his disappointment. His dream of playing professional hockey was about to come true.

The NHL was in the middle of a great change when Bobby joined the pro ranks. There had been just six teams in it for many years. But at the start of the 1967–68 season —while Bobby was still in Junior hockey—it was expanded to twelve teams. In the years to come, it would grow to eighteen teams.

Bobby knew that a great many fans were angry about the expansion. They said it was ruining the league. When there had been just six teams, there had been room for only the best players. But, with twelve teams, the need for players had doubled. There were men now in NHL uniforms who should never have gotten beyond the minors. Hockey games just weren't as good as they used to be.

And he knew that the fans were angry about something else. They thought the expansion was making a joke out of the postseason play-offs for the biggest prize in professional hockey, the Stanley Cup. The old teams had been able to keep most of their veteran players during the draft to build the expansion teams. The new teams had all been placed in the Western Division. Any new team that made it to the play-offs was sure to be beaten by one of the old teams with all its experienced players.

Finally, he knew that many fans were disgusted because expansion had changed the style of league play. Hockey had always been a rough game, but now it was rougher than ever before. Too rough. Too bruising and too violent. Club managers and coaches had found that violence could be used in place of skill in turning out a winning team.

Okay, Bobby thought. He'd show the fans that he definitely wasn't a minor leaguer. He'd work hard to help the Flyers win the Stanley Cup one day. As for the rough play—well, he'd take care of himself and his teammates out there on the ice.

The Philadelphia Flyers were an expansion team. They

had just finished their second season when Bobby was drafted. In its short history, the club had twice won a spot in the Stanley Cup play-offs. Both times, it had been quickly knocked out of contention by the very tough St. Louis Blues.

Because the Flyers were new in the NHL, Bobby knew little about them. In fact, the young Canadian didn't even know where Philadelphia was. He had to ask whether it was on the West or East Coast of the United States. He told friends that he felt a "little scared" when he thought about going to a city that he knew nothing about.

Vic Stasiuk was the Flyers' coach at the time. He was new to the job, having just been brought up from coaching in the club's farm system. It was up to him to decide whether Bobby would start professional play in the minor leagues or right at the top with the Flyers. The boy's performance in the Flyers' preseason training camp would tell the story.

Bobby reported to Quebec City, where the camp was located. Naturally, all new players are watched closely. But Bobby drew more attention than all the others put together. His diabetes made him a special case.

The Flyers still looked on the nineteen-year-old center from Flin Flon as a big gamble. Bobby, however, was confident. He showed his confidence by turning down Bud Poile's first contract offer: seven thousand dollars with a twenty-five-hundred-dollar bonus for the first season. Bobby held out for fourteen thousand dollars, with a five-thousand-dollar bonus. Poile finally agreed.

A few days after training began, however, Poile wondered if he had made a terrible mistake. Bobby fainted during a practice session.

This was the worst of signs, but Bobby came back the next day, working harder than ever. Stasiuk decided to try him at the center of a line with Lew Morrison, another promising rookie, and Reggie Fleming. Fleming was a veteran, a talkative man who would settle the rookies down.

The line clicked from the start. Stasiuk, an old-fashioned coach who expected hard work and no nonsense from his players, quickly recognized Bobby Clarke as a "comer." The coach liked everything about the young center's ability and attitude. It seemed that Bobby had earned a spot in the big leagues for his rookie year. Even the doubters were impressed. But then he fainted again during practice.

Bobby explained that these were the first times in three years that he had passed out. That didn't help much. It looked as if the demands of NHL hockey were simply too great for a diabetic.

By good luck, Frank Lewis, the club trainer, knew something about diabetes. He took Bobby aside for a talk and discovered that Bobby had been foolishly skipping his breakfasts. He had been coming to practice short of body energy.

Lewis made Bobby promise that he would never skip breakfast again. Then the trainer worked out a program that would supply Bobby with energy-building foods, foods that contained lots of sugar. Candy bars made Bobby thirsty when he played, so Lewis suggested a soft drink fortified with two tablespoons of sugar. Bobby agreed to drink this before each game or practice session. Then, when on the bench during games, Bobby was to sip sweet-ened orange juice. After a workout or game he had to drink a full glass of juice.

Bobby followed Lewis's program faithfully. There were no more problems. And Bobby performed so well at train-ing camp that Stasiuk had no choice but to take the rookie with him to Philadelphia for the 1969–70 season.

5

Never Satisfied

His friends from Flin Flon probably wouldn't have recognized Bobby when he first skated onto the ice in a Flyer uniform.

He was no longer a skinny kid with buck teeth and eyeglasses. He now had a compact, stocky build. His buck teeth had been knocked out long ago during Junior play. Now, when he removed his false teeth just before a game, there was a gap that stretched almost as wide as his smile. His eyeglasses had been replaced with contact lenses.

In the black-and-orange Flyer uniform, Bobby looked more like a real hockey player than ever before. But in action he had not changed much from his Junior years. He was still aggressive. He was still checking hard. He was still putting pressure on his opponents.

The big change was in the opponents themselves. They

were much different from the Junior players he had faced. They were pros. They were skillful and knew all the tricks. Many of them were just as aggressive as Bobby. He couldn't afford to make many mistakes.

In his first game, though, he did make a mistake, a serious one. The Flyers were up against the Minnesota North Stars. Bobby was eager to play, but when Stasiuk told him to go out on the ice, the rookie suddenly got the jitters. He had a right to them. This was, after all, his first appearance as a pro—the moment he had been dreaming about for most of his twenty years.

Suddenly, the puck shot his way. He got his stick on it and began an attack. But then Bill Goldsworthy swept in from the side. Before the rookie could stop him, Goldsworthy stole the puck and scored for the North Stars.

Bobby was surprised and bewildered, but he didn't let his poor start bother him. In fact, it may have been a good thing. It made Bobby try harder. After that, few opponents had an easy time trying a steal. When Bobby got the puck, he kept it under control.

The 1969–70 season was a good one for the young center. He appeared in all of the Flyers' seventy-six games. Stasiuk discovered early in the season that the entire team seemed to play better when Bobby was on the ice. His spirit, his effort, and his desire lifted everyone.

He gave the fans a lift, too. He brought a new excitement to the Flyer games. Attendance had been poor during the first two seasons at Philadelphia. But now ticket sales began to pick up. There were even some sellouts at the Spectrum, the Flyers' home rink.

Off the ice, the team discovered that Bobby was a nice

guy to have around. Early in the season, the fans voted Bobby "Flyer of the Month." The honor included a small cash award. Bobby would not accept the money. He asked that it be given instead to Warren Elliot, the club's assistant trainer, whose daughter needed an expensive operation.

Bobby's first-year statistics were not spectacular, but they were good, especially for a rookie. He scored 15 goals and had 31 assists for a total of 46 points. The numbers did not fully reflect his hard play, but they did put him in fourth place on the team's list of top scorers. And that, along with his aggressive style, won him the Rookie of the Year award in the NHL's Western Division.

The team record, however, was disappointing. The Flyers were in third place in their division until the last week in the season. Then they went into a scoring slump. The slump cost them a shot at the Stanley Cup because only the top three teams in each of the NHL's divisions could make it to the championship play-offs.

Still, there were good things about the season. Keith Allen, who replaced Bud Poile as general manager, declared that the team now had more muscle and scoring power than ever before. Allen was also pleased with attendance. The average gate for home games had passed the twelve-thousand mark for the first time in the club's history.

Bobby was credited for much of the improvement in both team play and attendance. With this kind of praise and the Rookie of the Year honor, he had the right to feel proud. And the right to celebrate.

Bobby, however, was shy and quiet away from home. It was not until he got back to Flin Flon for the summer break that he started to cut loose. He enjoyed going into the cafes and receiving the praise and attention of his friends. It was hard not to become a little cocky. He began playing the role of the NHL "hot shot."

Cockiness did not fit Bobby's character. Nevertheless, he might have gone right on playing the "hot shot" all summer had not something happened that made him think.

One night, he and friends went out to celebrate. They were speeding along in a car after having had a few drinks. Bobby was driving, and his reflexes were not as sharp as usual. He lost control when the wheels skidded on some loose gravel. The car shot off the road and flipped over.

The accident gave Bobby and his friends a bad scare. It was fortunate that no one was hurt. The next day, Bobby realized just how lucky they had been. He learned that another hockey player, Michel Briere of the Pittsburgh Penguins, a man Bobby had just beaten out for the Rookie of the Year award, was in a similar accident on the Quebec Highway.

Like Bobby, Briere lost control of his car. It crashed, and he was thrown through the windshield. Briere lay unconscious in a hospital for several weeks before he died.

Bobby was jolted. He said that Briere's death and his own accident caused him to look at a lot of things in life in a different way.

And he had another reason for looking at life differently. Her name was Sandra. She lived in Creighton, a small town near Flin Flon. She had been a cheerleader for the Bombers during Bobby's Junior years, and the two of them

46

had dated for a long time. Now, soon after the end of his rookie season, they were married.

From the start, Sandra Clarke was a steadying influence on Bobby. She had been around hockey players all her life. She did not look on them as gods, the way many a fan did. They were just regular people. They were in an unusual business, of course, but Sandra believed they should be treated like everyone else and be allowed to live normal lives.

She saw to it that Bobby never played the hockey "hot shot" again. She wanted her husband to be himself.

It may well have been Sandra's settling influence that helped Bobby overcome the "second-year jinx" in the 1970–71 season. The jinx is a very real thing. It has caused the downfall of many professional athletes in different sports.

An athlete will have an outstanding rookie year. He knows that he has to prove himself as a pro. And so he works doubly hard. He concentrates all the while. He turns in a star performance. He makes the grade and is praised by his teammates, the fans, and the press.

But then the second year comes along. There is not so much pressure. He no longer has to prove himself. He tends to let down. The result is a poor season. Some athletes never recover from the second-year jinx. But for the young center from Flin Flon, there was no problem.

Bobby set out to better his record in the 1970–71 season. He promised himself not to let the praise heaped on him in his rookie year go to his head. And he promised never to be satisfied with his performance on the ice. Let

47

the fans and his teammates remember his good plays. He would remember his mistakes and work to correct them.

These promises helped him face his second year like a seasoned pro—well, almost like a seasoned pro.

There was one important game against the Boston Bruins that made Bobby feel like a kid again. It was played in the Spectrum, and every one of the Flyers wanted a win for the hometown crowd. Flyer owner Ed Snider especially wanted the win because the Bruins had been walking all over his club for one season after another. The time had come to turn things around.

Before the game, Snider called the Flyers together. He told them that if they could knock off the Bruins, he would buy two new suits for each man. It was a generous offer. The Flyers were a fired-up team when they took to the ice.

Bobby gave the game everything he had. He hammered in two goals. He seemed to be all over the ice. But it wasn't enough. The Bruins were just too tough. They took the game by one goal.

When the final buzzer sounded, Bobby could not help himself. He broke down and cried before he could skate off the ice. The tears that streaked his face embarrassed him. He held his head down, hoping the fans would not notice. But they did notice. And they tried to cheer him up.

"That's okay, Bobby."

"You'll get 'em next time, kid."

"Good game, Clarke. Hang in there."

The fan support helped, but crying over a loss was not the professional thing to do. At least, Bobby didn't think so. He was hard on himself all through the season. He drove himself. He was never satisfied.

In a scramble, the puck flies up in front of Bobby's face as the Red Wing goalie wonders what has happened to his defensemen. *(Photo: Clifton Boutelle)*

Bobby shoots, stares, and keeps moving forward. Even on long shots, there may be a chance for a rebound. (*Photo: Clifton Boutelle*)

Along with agility, Bobby can put power into his stride. It's the combination of agility and power that makes him a top playmaker in the NHL. *(Photo: Clifton Boutelle)*

Bobby uses his stick as a reminder. Opponents never forget him when he is on their trail. *(Photo: Clifton Boutelle)*

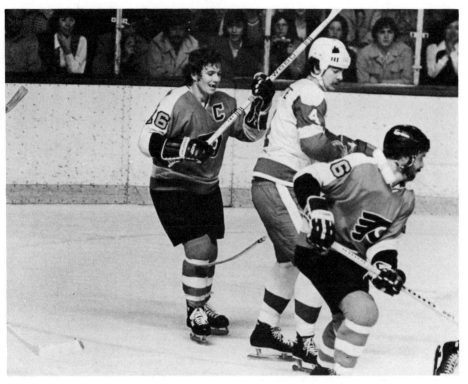

After making his pass, Bobby follows the crowd as the Flyers work the puck toward the goal in this game against Detroit. *(Photo: Clifton Boutelle)*

Bobby keeps his eyes on the puck as he moves into position for a pass. (*Photo: Clifton Boutelle*)

Flyers' coach Fred Shero prepares to drink a ginger ale toast to Bobby's Most Valuable Player award in 1973. It was the first of three MVPs for Bobby so far in his career. *(Photo: United Press International)*

Heavy traffic doesn't bother Bobby. Here he weaves around sticks to win the race for the puck. *(Photo: Clifton Boutelle)*

He ended the year with 27 goals and 36 assists—a total of 63 points. That was up 17 points over his rookie year. He had overcome the second-year jinx. More important, he had helped the Flyers make the play-offs for the Stanley Cup.

The Flyers finished third in their division, just good enough for a play-off spot. Unfortunately, their opponent for the first round was the Chicago Black Hawks, an old, established club, a strong team.

The Black Hawks swept the series in four games, 5–2, 6–2, 3–2, and 6–2. During most of the play, Bobby was matched against Stan Mikita, the Hawks' veteran forward. Bobby had to face a hard fact: Mikita outplayed him every step of the way. When Mikita was on the ice, Bobby rarely got his stick on the puck. It was a humbling experience. It drove Bobby to remember a promise he had made to himself when he first joined the Flyers.

Not one of the expansion teams had ever won the Stanley Cup. Bobby told himself that the Flyers would be the first one to bring the Cup home. It would take hard work. He was ready for it.

6

NHL Star

Long before the end of Bobby's second season with the team, the Flyers were unhappy with Vic Stasiuk. He was an excellent coach who gave everything he had to the game. But he had one great problem.

The players felt that he was much too strict with them. He seemed to treat them more like young amateurs than highly paid professionals. When he thought that they were not doing their best, he quickly took away team privileges. Once he even ordered a soft-drink machine removed from the dressing room.

Actions such as these caused much grumbling among the players right from the start of the 1970–71 season. Reporters soon picked up the grumbling and wrote that the Philadelphia club was one of the unhappiest teams in hockey. This sort of talk alarmed the Flyers' management. It could hurt attendance. Something had to be done.

General manager Keith Allen decided that Stasiuk must go. As soon as the season ended, he removed the coach and replaced him with Fred Shero.

Stasiuk was surprised, but not bitter. He even praised the man chosen to take his place. Fred Shero had coached for many years in the New York Rangers' farm system. He was an ex-boxer who had a reputation for turning out fighting teams.

Shero really shook the Flyers up when they began to practice for the 1971–72 season. Sometimes he had them work out with a tennis ball instead of a puck. Skipping wildly all over the ice, it did much to sharpen their reflexes. To build their stamina, he made them bunny hop up and down the rink to loud music. He spent long hours working with individual players and helping them to better their game.

There was never a dull moment when the new coach was around. Gone was Stasiuk's iron discipline. Shero encouraged the players to argue with him if they thought that any of his ideas for practicing and playing were wrong. He felt that men who were given the chance to voice their opinions played better in the long run.

And he did not take away team privileges if someone let down. Nor did he fine the offender. He simply parked him on the bench for a few days. This embarrassed the player and made him eager to get back on the ice and do his best.

By the start of the 1971–72 season, Shero had all the Flyers behind him. They felt that a championship team was in the making, one that could really take the Stanley Cup. Then, early in the season, the coach did one more thing to weld the club solidly together. He named a new team captain.

Defenseman Ed Van Imp had captained the Flyers ever since the club's beginnings. He was a veteran player, a steady man who was good at helping and encouraging his teammates to their best play. But he had never been comfortable as captain, and so he now asked Shero to let him step down.

Shero agreed. With Van Imp's help, he looked around, sighted the leadership abilities in Bobby Clarke, and named the third-year center as the new team captain. Bobby, who was just twenty-three years old, became the youngest captain in the history of the NHL.

Led by Shero and Bobby, the Flyers put in a fine season, despite a tragic setback. Their excellent goalie, Bruce Gamble, suffered a heart attack during a game with the Canucks at Vancouver and had to retire from hockey. But even then, it looked as if the Flyers might get a shot at the Stanley Cup play-offs. As the season rolled to an end, they were racing with the St. Louis Blues and the Pittsburgh Penguins to nail down the third-place spot in their division. The race was not decided until the very last game on the Flyers' schedule.

The Flyers went up against the Buffalo Sabres that night. A win or a tie for the Philadelphia club would assure a play-off spot. But a loss would end the season right then and there.

Bobby worked the puck down the ice to score in the first period. Teammate Rick Foley followed suit in the second. With a 2–0 lead, the Flyers were jubilant. An easy win seemed assured. But the Sabres had other ideas. Soon after Foley's score, they drove the puck in for a tally of their own and then tied things in the final period.

Shero wanted to preserve the tie. It would be as good as a win so far as getting into the play-offs was concerned. He ordered his men to play a tight defensive game. The strategy worked, right up to the final ten seconds. It was then that the Sabres' Gerry Meehan, who had once played for the Flyers, received a perfect pass at center ice and rushed toward the Philadelphia goal. Van Imp backed slowly, trying to slow the rush. Meehan took a desperate, last-ditch shot. Goalie Doug Favell never saw the puck until it sailed by his right knee and into the net. Van Imp had screened his vision. The game ended 3–2, with the Flyers out of the play-offs.

Although disappointed with the loss, Bobby could be happy with his record for the season. He toted up 35 goals and 46 assists for a total of 81 points. No Flyer had ever racked up that many points in a single season.

He also showed that the role of team leader suited him and the Flyers perfectly. Coach Shero was pleased. He called Bobby the greatest active player in professional hockey.

Shero wasn't alone in his opinion. On June 7, 1972, Bobby Clarke was named the winner of the Bill Masterton Memorial Trophy. The award is presented each year to the player "who best exemplifies the qualities of perseverance, sportsmanship, and dedication to hockey."

There was no question about it now. Bobby Clarke was an NHL star.

Naturally, Bobby was happy to become the first Flyer

ever to win a major hockey award. But another honor soon followed, one that pleased him even more. He was chosen to play for Team Canada in an upcoming series against the Soviet National Hockey Club. The Canadian squad was to represent its country in an eight-game battle with the top team in Europe.

Team Canada was coached by Harry Sinden, the long-time coach of the Boston Bruins. He was given a free hand in choosing his players, and he picked the very best he could find. On the team with Bobby were Phil and Tony Esposito, Ken Dryden, Josh Guèvremont, Gil Perreault, J. P. Parise, Jean Ratelle, Gary Bergman, Rod Gilbert, Serge Savard, Yvan Cournoyer, Dennis Hull, Vic Hadfield, Frank Mahovlich, Rick Martin, Ron Ellis, Paul Henderson, and Brad Park.

Many of these men were players whom Bobby had admired since his days of Tom Thumb hockey. He was thrilled to be on the same team with them. And it certainly looked as if the Soviets would be overpowered by such stars.

Nearly every hockey fan in North America thought so. There were some who figured that the Soviets would be trounced so badly that they would never want to play the Canadians again.

Even Sinden, who knew the Soviets' skillful style, believed that his team would dominate. The Soviets were excellent passers and liked to work the puck in close to the net before shooting. The Canadians, on the other hand, liked to shoot early and then charge in for rebounds. The games, thus, would give an interesting contrast in styles. But Sinden believed that the Canadian style would produce more goals because of superior goaltending. No one could match Canadian goalies. And so, if the Canadians took more shots than the Soviets, they would surely get more goals. It was that simple.

As it worked out, it was not so simple. Most of the experts overlooked Team Canada's most serious handicap: The Soviet players had been working together for months, even years; Sinden's team would have just a few days of practice before the series began.

Sinden was worried about this, but much of the worry faded early in the practice sessions when he put Bobby Clarke at the center of a line with Ron Ellis and Paul Henderson. The three played as if they had been skating together all their lives.

True, one good forward line did not make a winning team, but Sinden and his players felt confident as the opening day of the series approached. The first game would be played on September 2, 1972, in the Forum at Montreal.

7

The Soviet Series

Team Canada jumped to a 2–0 lead early in the first game. The sellout crowd buzzed excitedly. Who could doubt that the Canadians were going to flatten the Soviets in all eight meetings?

It turned out, however, that the Soviet National Hockey Club was just a little slow in getting started. When the visitors finally put their offense together, they were able to flash right through the Canadian defense time and again. They outplayed their hosts in every way. They even topped them at goaltending. The result: a whopping 7–3 loss for Team Canada.

The defeat stunned the North American hockey world.

Bobby Clarke was depressed. It was bad enough that his teammates had worked together for such a short time. Now another weakness had been exposed: The Canadians were

61

out of shape after a summer layoff from NHL play. They couldn't keep pace with the well-trained and well-conditioned Soviets.

Depressed though he was, Bobby didn't give up. His men would become physically fit in a few games. He'd just have to hope that it wouldn't be too late by then. He even managed a smile when he told reporters that the Soviets had wanted to play the series so that they could learn about hockey from the professionals.

So far, he grinned, the only thing the professionals had shown them was that you have to be in shape to play hockey. That was something that the Soviets already knew.

In the second game, Team Canada made up for the loss by downing the Soviets 4–1. The score, however, didn't tell the whole story. It was not an easy victory. The Canadian skaters left the rink exhausted. They were still in too poor a shape for the kind of hockey that the series demanded.

The poor conditioning showed itself again in the third game. Team Canada took a 3–1 lead and then failed to protect it. The Soviets counterattacked with such skill and strength that the Canadians felt lucky to leave the ice with a 4–4 tie.

The teams now stood even, with a win apiece and the tie. The Canadian fans thought it was a very poor record. When Team Canada skated out for the fourth game, which was played in Vancouver's Pacific Coliseum, the crowd of eighteen thousand began to boo. The booing continued for the rest of the night.

Bobby and his teammates were stunned. They expected to be jeered during NHL road games. The booing was all a part of professional hockey and all really done in good fun.

But this was different. Now they represented their nation. Their own countrymen were down on them. It hurt.

For their part, the fans felt that they had been cheated. The newspapers had led them to believe that their team was invincible. The press had drawn too good a picture of the team, and they didn't like it.

Despite the booing, the Canadians played hard. But the Soviets seemed to be improving with each game. They knew Team Canada's weaknesses now, and they took full advantage of them. They skated to a 5–3 victory.

As if things weren't bad enough, the Canadian press began blasting the Team Canada players. Sportswriters and broadcasters accused them of not trying. Bobby Clarke was one of the few to escape criticism. Some writers even praised him for his skill and tireless effort.

Bobby, however, came in for some criticism from the Soviets. They didn't like Team Canada's rough style of play, and they pointed to Clarke as the roughest man on the team. "Boo-by Clarke is a no-no," was the English phrase that all the Soviets learned before they went home to continue the series in Moscow.

The Canadians were in low spirits when they flew to Moscow, but Bobby was still hopeful. He hated to see his teammates blasted in the press, but his own escape from criticism had boosted his confidence. Before the series, he had secretly felt that he had really no business being on this star-studded team. Now he knew that he belonged and that he could do much for Team Canada.

The first game on Soviet soil, however, gave his confidence a nasty jolt. Team Canada grabbed an early 4–1 lead, but again the Soviets surged back. Making a shambles of the Canadian defense, they tied the score at 4–4 in the final period.

Trying desperately to get an offense started, Bobby flew after the puck as it was bouncing wildly near the boards. He managed to get his stick on it and sent it skidding back to teammate Rod Seiling. The pass was a bad one. The puck flashed wide of Seiling. Valery Kharlamov, who had been making the Canadians look silly all night, intercepted and sent a perfect cross to Vladimir Ivanovich Vikulov. Vikulov nudged the puck into the net to give the Soviets a 5–4 victory.

After five games, the Soviet Union led the series with three wins and a tie against Team Canada's one win and tie. Just three more games remained. Some of the Canadian players began to wonder if things could get any worse. They got their answer before the next game. It was "Yes."

Four of their teammates quit. Josh Guèvremont, Gil Perreault, Rick Martin, and Vic Hadfield all packed up and went home. They told reporters that they had not been given enough time on the ice to do any good for Team Canada.

Coach Sinden was furious. He compared the four to rats that jumped off a ship because they thought it was sinking. Sinden, with strong support from NHL scoring ace Phil Esposito, spread the word: The ship was not about to sink.

Meanwhile, fans back home began giving Team Canada the support it deserved. Telegrams poured in to the team's Moscow headquarters, more than fifty thousand of them. They all said the same thing: Canada's pulling for you. You can come fighting back, win three games in a row, and take the series. Good luck.

Most Soviet fans, however, felt that Team Canada

hadn't a chance of coming back. Strangely enough, one of the few who still looked on the visitors as a threat was Vsevolod Brobrov, coach of the Soviet team. He knew that the Canadians had been out of condition during the early games. He knew that they had been overconfident and undertrained. But that was all gone now. Brobrov warned his players that the three final games might be the toughest they had ever played.

He was right.

The Soviets not only dropped the next game—the sixth —by a tight 3–2 score, but they also lost the heart of their offense. Valery Kharlamov, who had intercepted Bobby's pass in the first Moscow battle, had been outskating the Canadians all through the series. Now he went too far with the young center. During a scramble for the puck, he dug the end of his stick into Bobby's stomach. Though Bobby was doubled over with pain, no penalty was called. Bobby's anger flared. Something had to be done to slow this guy Kharlamov down.

A few seconds later, Kharlamov started racing the puck up the ice, with Bobby pursuing close behind. This sort of thing had happened too often, Bobby decided. Using both hands, he swung his stick hard. It caught Kharlamov's ankle. The Soviet cried out, went down in a heap, and had to be helped off the ice. Bobby was penalized two minutes for slashing. Kharlamov was out for the rest of the series with a chipped bone in his ankle.

Many hockey fans still believe that the loss of Kharlamov turned the series around. They may be right. The next two games were certainly close ones. They could have gone either way. A healthy Kharlamov might have changed the outcome.

65

The seventh game was tied 3–3 until the final three minutes. Then Paul Henderson, Bobby's linemate, scored the winning goal. The victory tied the series.

In the eighth and deciding game, Team Canada trailed 5–3 at the opening of the final period. For the millions of fans following the action on television and radio, the Soviets seemed to be in full command. But Phil Esposito tied things up with a goal and an assist. The tie held until the last sixty seconds. Then Esposito took the puck again. He was forced wide. In desperation, he shot the puck hard at the Soviet net. The goalie blocked it. But it rebounded to Henderson. Henderson pumped it into the net just before the final buzzer sounded.

The 6–5 victory gave Team Canada the series. The Canadians went home with a record of four wins, three losses, and one tie. There had been some spectacular plays on both sides, but the play that earned the most attention was Bobby Clarke's two-handed attack on Kharlamov.

Bobby told reporters that he was not proud of what he had done. But he was not ashamed either. He said that the Soviets played just as dirty as anyone else at times. He felt there was just one difference: The Canadians play dirty out in the open. The Soviets are sneaky about it.

Bobby stressed, however, that the series had produced some excellent hockey. Rough play was getting far too much attention. The Soviets, Bobby said, were great hockey players. He would like to meet them again one day.

To that he added one more point: Whether or not he ever faced the Soviet club on the ice again, he'd never forget the series of September 1972.

8

Bid for Glory

Many of the Team Canada players went into slumps when they returned to their NHL teams for the 1972–73 season. After the Soviet challenge, they felt let down. But not Bobby.

This was to be his fourth season in NHL hockey. He planned to make it his best yet.

The season began on a happy note for him. His wife, Sandra, gave birth to a son, the first of their two children. The family moved from an apartment to a spacious home. Bobby knew that Sandra had always been lonely when he was away on road trips. Now, with a home and a new baby to care for, she would be too busy to be lonely.

Though it started happily, the season turned into a difficult one for Bobby. The World Hockey Association had just been formed. It was represented in Philadelphia by the Blazers. Bobby knew that the Flyers would have to work hard to keep from losing many of their fans to the new team.

The Blazers attempted to lure the fans away with a publicity campaign against Bobby. Derek Sanderson, who had been a star center for the Boston Bruins, had jumped over to the WHA for a big pay increase and was now playing for the Blazers. The Blazers claimed that he was a better man than Bobby. Why watch Clarke when you can watch Sanderson and the Blazers? the club asked again and again for all to hear.

Sanderson was indeed a good player. But he loved publicity. And he loved to talk. He was quick to begin criticizing Bobby in the newspapers.

Bobby wanted no part of a public argument and kept his mouth shut. As it turned out, he didn't have to say a thing. Sanderson proved to be his own worst enemy. He talked so much that even the Blazer fans grew sick of hearing him. He was out for a time with a back injury, but he had become so unpopular by then that his team wouldn't use him when he returned. He went back to the Bruins just as the Blazers were finishing off a disastrous season.

In the meantime, the Flyers were putting in a great season. They were in second place in their division and battling hard to reach the Stanley Cup play-offs. Games that year were just about as rough as Bobby had ever seen.

Much of the roughness was due to Dave Schultz, a player new to the Flyers. He quickly became known as the NHL's toughest fighter. "The Hammer," as he was called, set a game pattern for the Flyers that shook the entire league. It was rugged hockey and not always the best kind. But it certainly helped a team to win.

If an opposing player roughed up a Flyer, Schultz wanted revenge right away. He was at the center of many slugfests and wrestling matches. He won most of them. Teams throughout the league began to think twice before picking on any Flyer.

So rough did the Flyers play that some games nearly turned into riots. In Vancouver, the team attacked the Canuck fans after one angry spectator reached over the rail and pulled rookie Don Saleski's hair. Once peace was restored, the game went on to a 4–4 tie. The Flyers returned later in the season and trounced the Canucks, 10–5.

Then there was the game with the Detroit Red Wings. Four major fights broke out on the ice, and there was a total of 134 minutes of penalty time, a league record. It was during that game that Gary Bergman, a big Red Wing defenseman, made the mistake of attacking Bobby Clarke. Bobby's linemates, Bill Barber and Bill Flett, rushed to his aid with flying fists. But no Red Wings arrived to help Bergman. That, Bobby said later, showed the difference in spirit between the two teams.

Bobby tallied up a fine record for the season. In all, he played in 78 games. He scored 37 goals and had 67 assists for a total of 104 points. In one game—a 7–6 win over the Montreal Canadiens—he scored a 3-goal hat trick.

As good as his record was, Bobby was not the only Flyer with scoring punch. Rookie Rick MacLeish became the youngest player in the NHL to score 50 goals in a season. He was just 21 years old.

The Flyers ended the season in their second-place spot and earned a crack at the Stanley Cup. They entered the play-offs with high hopes. Maybe this was the year that they would bring the Cup home.

The play-offs began at the Spectrum and pitted the Flyers against the Minnesota North Stars. For a few frightening moments, Bobby thought that the first game might be his last. During the opening action, a teammate's stick accidentally hit him in the eye. His contact lens shattered.

Bobby fell to the ice, banging his skates in pain. "I can't see! I can't see!" he yelled.

He was rushed to the hospital, where doctors removed the lens fragments. The eyeball and eyelid had been scratched, but there was no permanent damage. Bobby, wearing soft contact lenses, was back on the ice for the second game.

It was a lucky break for the Flyers. They had lost the first game, but Bobby now helped them to a 4–1 win. They played three more games and knocked the North Stars out of the play-offs.

Then it was on to the semifinal series with the Montreal Canadiens. Here was a team that always roused Bobby to his angry best, because the Montreal coach was forever knocking the Flyers in the newspapers. Bobby found himself matched against Henri "Pocket Rocket" Richard, the club's leading player.

The two opponents played hard and expertly. Their match turned out to be a pretty even one. But, still, the Flyers were in trouble. They were exhausted after their battles with the North Stars. Montreal was a powerhouse

Bobby and goalie Bernie Parent (right) carry the Stanley Cup off the crowded ice of the Spectrum after the Flyers beat the Boston Bruins, 1–0, in the 1973–74 championship playoffs. *(Photo: United Press International)*

Nothing tastes as good as victory, but champagne out of the Stanley Cup tastes all right to Bobby as he toasts the end of the Flyers' spectacular 1973–74 season. *(Photo: United Press International)*

You almost have to foul Bobby Clarke to stop him. Halfhearted stick taps like this do nothing to slow him down. *(Photo: Clifton Boutelle)*

Even when he's blocked out of the play, Bobby's eyes follow the action. (*Photo: Clifton Boutelle*)

The Flyers take the Stanley Cup for the second time in a row. Here, NHL president Clarence Campbell presents the Cup to (from left) Bernie Parent, Bobby Clarke, and Bill Clement. *(Photo: United Press International)*

Once again, the two stars, Bernie Parent and Bobby Clarke, carry the Cup from the rink after beating the Buffalo Sabres, 2–0. (*Photo: United Press International*)

All-time great Maurice Richard presents the Hart Trophy to Bobby during the 1976 awards dinner at Montreal. It was the third time Bobby came out on top in the Most Valuable Player vote to take the award. *(Photo: United Press International)*

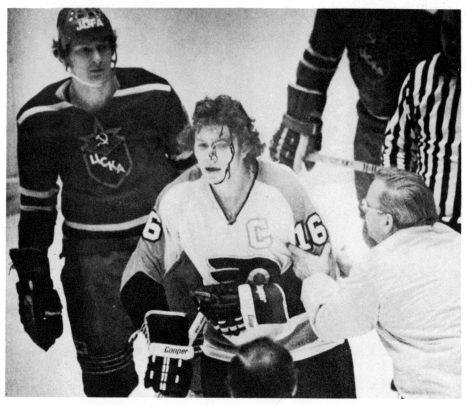

Bobby leaves the ice with a facial cut in the third period of the Flyers' game against the Soviet Army team on January 11, 1976. The Flyers won, 4–1. *(Photo: United Press International)*

club. The Flyers fell behind right at the start and never caught up. They lost the series, four games to one.

Though the Flyers were out of the play-offs, the city of Philadelphia gave them a tumultuous welcome on their return from Montreal. The club had gotten into the semifinals, and that seemed good enough for the fans. But Bobby was greatly disappointed. He could think of just one thing. He and his team had failed to go all the way to the Cup.

Okay, he told himself, next year is just around the corner. We'll come fighting back—twice as hard.

Despite his disappointment, the 1972–73 season was not a complete loss for Bobby. The Professional Hockey Writers' Association voted him the NHL's Most Valuable Player award and he thus was given the coveted Hart Trophy. Bobby received 158 votes. Phil Esposito followed with 96. Bobby Orr had 63.

Bobby Clarke was dazed by the honor. He couldn't believe that he had been chosen. He said that he did not know why the hockey writers had picked him.

Everyone else knew, though. He had earned the award hands down.

9

The Stanley Cup

The 1973–74 season began with Bobby remembering his old promise: The Flyers would become the first NHL expansion team to bring home the Stanley Cup.

They had come closer than ever before last season. The team had changed very little since then. This was the year for going all the way. Bobby was sure of it. So were his teammates.

But there was a problem: The Flyers were weak in one area—the goalkeeper's spot. There they made an important change.

Young Bernie Parent had been their backup goalie at one time. He had left to play a season with the Toronto Maple Leafs and then had gone on to the Blazers in the WHA. Now the Flyers brought him back.

He had been a good goalie in his earlier days. But now

he had become an extraordinary performer. The Flyers watched him on the ice and couldn't believe that he was the same man. Parent credited his improvement to his year with the Leafs when he had shared goaltending duties with his hero, Jacques Plante. Plante, who was nearing the end of a long career, had never stopped coaching him.

With Parent guarding the net, the Flyers posted a spectacular season. By October, they had a firm grip on first place in their division. They never let go. They went on to record 50 wins, 16 losses, and 12 ties. Only four other teams in NHL history had ever won 50 games in one season.

The Flyers also put another record into the books. It wasn't one to be proud of. Playing harder than ever, they racked up a total of 1,750 penalty minutes. The total was 603 minutes above the previous record for a club in a single season.

But no matter. The Flyers had finished first in their division, the first time they had ever done so. They were in the Stanley Cup play-offs.

Their first opponent was the Atlanta Flames, a new club in the ever-growing NHL. The Flyers were heavily favored to take the opening series, but they knew that the Atlanta team was well coached and well conditioned. And so the Flyers took no chances. They played hard. No one let down. The Flames were knocked out in four straight games.

The victories took Bobby and his teammates into the semifinal series to meet the New York Rangers. Now the Flyers found themselves the underdogs. The sports reporters pointed out that Philadelphia had never before made it beyond the semifinals. The Rangers were as tough as any outfit on ice. They were favored not only to take the semifinals but also the Cup itself.

One of the Rangers' greatest strengths was center Walt Tkaczuk. He was said to be as good as Bobby Clarke, if not better. Ranger coach Emile Francis told his players that the best way to stop Philadelphia was to stop Bobby. Francis was counting on Tkaczuk to do the job.

The Flyers, however, quickly upset New York's plans. Early in the first game, Bobby and teammate André "Moose" Dupont turned up ice beside Tkaczuk. The three raced along together for a few feet. Then Moose bumped against Bobby and sent him crashing into Tkaczuk. Bobby's shoulder struck Tkaczuk's head. The Ranger center fell like a rock. Later, Bobby insisted it had been an accident.

Accident or not, Tkaczuk left the ice glassy-eyed and was benched for the night. The Flyers took a 4–0 victory.

Tkaczuk returned for the second game. He brought with him two things: a helmet and a bad temper. He and Bobby tangled at once. Fists flew, and both men were sent to the penalty box. They went back to the box twice again before the game ended in a 5–2 win for the Flyers.

The first two games were played at Philadelphia. When the series now moved to New York, a miracle seemed to be in the making. If the underdog Flyers could go on winning, they could sweep the semifinals. But the Rangers, inspired by their hometown fans, came fighting back into contention. They took the next two games, 5–3 and 2–1. They did so by matching the Flyers' hard style of play.

So bruising was the action that two Flyers were hospitalized. Bob "Hound Dog" Kelly left the ice with torn ligaments. And Barry Ashbee went out with an eye injury when he blocked a Ranger shot with his face. Tragically, the injury ended Ashbee's playing career.

The teams were back in the Spectrum for the fifth game. The Flyers managed a 4–1 win, but they seemed to be running out of gas. They were obviously tired. They had lost two of their men. The fans—and the Rangers—began to wonder if the Philadelphians could keep up the bruising play forever. Then the Rangers won the sixth game and tied the series up at three apiece.

Back in their dressing room after the sixth game, the Rangers celebrated. They were sure that the Flyers were finished and that one more game would see them dumped out of the play-offs. As it turned out, the New Yorkers were too sure. The Flyers came out fighting mad for the seventh game. They overcame a 1–1 tie in the first period and then slowly crept ahead. They stayed ahead to post a 4–3 win.

They had won four games. They had taken the semifinals.

The Philadelphia fans went wild. For the first time in its history, their team had made the finals in Stanley Cup competition. Now could the Flyers go all the way? Could they beat the powerful Boston Bruins, a team with two superstars—Phil Esposito and Bobby Orr?

Flyer coach Fred Shero believed that they could. The Bruins were the heavy favorites, but he had long felt that Esposito and Orr carried the whole team. If only his men could stop those two, he was pretty sure the Boston club would come apart at the seams.

Shero studied films of past Flyer-Bruin games. He decided that his team had always made life too easy for

Esposito and Orr. The Flyers had always checked each man with just one player. Shero now planned to send the entire forward line against them.

This, he said, would force the Bruin attack to the outside. They'd have to change their whole style of play.

The first game in the final series was played in Boston Garden. Shero's plan worked for most of the night. The Flyers held Esposito firmly in check and kept the score tied 2–2 until the final seconds. But then Orr broke into the open with the puck. He flashed up to the Flyer net and shot the puck in to give Boston a 3–2 win.

The Bruins then looked as if they were going to take the second game as well. They forged ahead at 2–1 and stayed there until, again, there were just seconds left. Now it was Moose Dupont's turn to be a hero. He drove the puck into the Boston net, tied the score, and sent the game into overtime.

The Bruins immediately launched a powerful attack, but Bernie Parent blocked every shot. Then Bobby Clarke got his stick on the puck and staged a one-man show that stunned the crowd. He skated the puck into the Bruin zone and fired a long shot. The puck rebounded off the Boston goalie. Bobby was there to flip the rebound into the net. The triumphant Flyers skated off the ice with the series tied at one each.

The next four games were scheduled for Philadelphia. Shero was a happy man when he returned home. His Flyers were following his plan and doing well. Though Orr was still a threat, Esposito was being held in check. And the Flyers now had the advantage of home ice. They also had a good-luck charm.

It was a recording of "God Bless America," with the

words sung by the great radio and television star, Kate Smith. It was played before the start of all important home games.

The song had been heard 36 times at the Spectrum, and the Flyers had followed it with a whopping 34 wins to just 1 loss and 1 tie. The recording was not played at all home games, but many Philadelphia fans said it should be. It certainly seemed to lift the Flyers. And it seemed to jinx their opponents.

The jinx worked again. The Bruins dropped the third game, 4–1. The fourth game was a little tighter. But it was still another win for the Flyers, this time by a 4–2 margin.

Three wins in a row put the Flyers in firm control of the series. One more victory would take the Cup. But the Bruins were now used to Shero's game plan. In the fifth game, they threw a vicious attack against the Flyers. It broke Orr loose, and the Bruins trounced the Philadelphians, 5–1.

Suddenly the pressure was on the Flyers. They had to win the sixth game and take the Cup right away. A Bruin victory, tying things up at three apiece, would send the series back to Boston. If that happened, the Bruins would have the advantage of home ice during the final, deciding game.

But the Flyers had an ace up their sleeves. They played it. Kate Smith, knowing of the good luck that her recording had always brought the team, agreed to appear in person at the Spectrum to sing "God Bless America."

It was stunning. Miss Smith stood on the ice. She was bathed in the blue glow of spotlights. Her strong, sure voice reached to the Spectrum rafters. When the final note faded, there was a long moment of silence before the crowd burst into applause.

Even the Bruins were moved by the performance. Orr and Esposito skated over and shook Miss Smith's hand. Perhaps they hoped to bring some luck their way.

As it turned out, nothing depended on luck. The game was decided by good play. First, there was the face-off that Flyer Rick MacLeish won in the Bruin zone about halfway through the first period. He sent the puck to Moose Dupont, and Dupont shot it toward the net. The shot was a weak one that the Boston goalie could have handled easily. But MacLeish flashed across the goalmouth and deflected the puck into the net.

Next, there was the fine play of Bernie Parent. The MacLeish score gave the Flyers a 1–0 edge, but it also spurred the Bruins to an all-out attack. Orr broke free of his coverage and was all over the ice. He shot at the net time and again. But he couldn't get the puck past the determined Parent.

Sometimes Bernie stopped the puck with spectacular dives. Sometimes he met it head-on with his legs and shoulders. Sometimes he whacked it away with his stick. The Flyer goalie held the Bruins scoreless and saved the game until the steam began to go out of the attack.

Then there was the way that Bobby Clarke battled Orr. The 1–0 lead began to look very big as the final period began. Orr continued to attack fiercely. His teammates were tired, and he was now the Bruins' last hope. But Clarke kept getting in his way, checking hard and pressing close. He kept refusing to give Orr the skating room that the Bruin needed to break free for the goal.

Finally, with less than three minutes left on the clock, Clarke stole the puck from Orr and started up ice. Orr, in a rare loss of temper, stopped him with a flying tackle that sent both men crashing to the ice. The Bruin scoring ace was sent to the penalty box for two minutes. Boston's hopes died.

The final seconds melted away with the fans chanting the count—FIVE, FOUR, THREE, TWO, ONE! Then it was all over.

The Flyers had won the game, the finals, and the Stanley Cup. The fans screamed and danced in the stands and tried to climb out on the ice. The Flyers rushed to embrace Parent. They crowded about him, leaping high and pounding him on the back. Some slipped and fell on the ice. Some laughed. Some cried. Parent was buried under a mound of orange-and-black jerseys.

A few minutes later, when some order had been restored, the victorious Flyers went skating around the rink. Leading them were Parent and Bobby. Held high between the two players was the huge, silver Stanley Cup.

Even then, many of the spectators couldn't believe what they were seeing. Was it all a dream? Or had the Philadelphia Flyers really become the first expansion team in NHL history to win hockey's top prize?

10

Was It a Fluke?

The people of Philadelphia jammed the streets. They cheered. They sang. They cried. Waving Flyer pennants, they formed parades on the spur of the moment. The celebration continued all night and all the next day.

The Flyers gave a night-long victory party. The players weren't able to head home for some well-earned rest until dawn. Bobby, however, could get no sleep. He found a crowd of happy, unruly fans in front of his house. They made so much noise and stayed for so long that the Clarke family had to move to a motel before Bobby was able to fall into bed.

Philadelphia didn't return to normal for several days. The fans needed several days to get it into their heads that a wild dream had come true. But even then, there were many who still couldn't believe what had happened. Had the Flyers just been lucky? Or had their victory been a real one?

Bernie Parent, named the Most Valuable Player in the final series, had no doubts. If the team stuck together, he said, it would be a threat for years to come. All the Flyers agreed, but they knew it would be tough to retain the Cup the next year. Every outfit in the NHL would be gunning for them in the 1974–75 season.

Bobby started the new season with a contract that guaranteed him fifty thousand dollars a year until he was age forty-five. He must have smiled when he signed the contract. This was pretty good for someone whose Tom Thumb coach had once pegged as an average skater. And someone who had been passed up in the draft by so many teams because he had diabetes.

As a matter of fact, hardly anyone in the NHL now ever thought of Bobby's diabetes. He had shown long ago that the illness couldn't stand in the way of a man with ambition and determination. There were many people outside the league, however, who did remember the illness. They said that Bobby was an inspiration to young people everywhere who suffered the same problem. Bobby modestly brushed such compliments aside.

The new season saw him again prove himself a fine team captain. He was consulted about team trades and helped to make some good ones, among them the deal that brought winger Reggie Leach to Philadelphia. Bobby also worked with any Flyer who went into a scoring slump. Often he would change his line to include the slumping player. Then he would set the man up for so many goal shots that the player quickly regained his confidence.

Though playing hard, the Flyers did not dominate their division in 1974–75 as they had the year before. But they headed for the finish with a firm hold on second place.

Coach Shero was ready to settle for the second-place spot. It would put the Flyers into the Cup play-offs. And it would give him the chance to use some players who had warmed the bench for most of the season. Without the pressure of battling for first place, he could give these men some valuable playing experience.

Bobby objected. The Flyers were out to show that their win of the previous season hadn't been a fluke. They should try for first place. He said that the benched players had told him that they wanted a first-place finish more than some time on the ice.

Shero nodded. Okay. The Flyers would go all out.

They did just that. They put on a final drive that lifted them to the division's top spot. Winger Reggie Leach took the team scoring honors for the season, whacking in 45 goals. Bobby followed with 27 goals and 89 assists, for a total of 116 points. His assists set a new NHL record for a single season.

Thanks to the all-out finish, the Flyers entered the Cup play-offs a hot team. They knocked out the powerful Toronto Maple Leafs in the opening round and then took three straight games from the New York Islanders in the semifinals. The Islanders, however, had a reputation as a comeback team. As if working some magic, they overpowered the Flyers and tied the series at three games apiece.

Bobby knew that magic had nothing to do with it. He could see that suddenly his teammates just weren't doing their best. He started bawling them out for sloppy play and poor effort. Among those who felt his anger was Rick MacLeish. MacLeish answered by scoring a three-goal hat trick in the final game with the Islanders. The Flyers won the game, 4-1, and advanced to the finals.

The Flyers now went against the Buffalo Sabres. The Sabres had "the French Connection," a forward line made up of Gilbert Perreault, Richard Martin, and René Robert. The line had scored an amazing 131 points during the season. But Shero believed it was a line that could be stopped. He told Bobby to break up the "Connection."

Bobby did just what Shero wished. He broke up the "Connection" by staying close to Perreault and bottling him up while his Flyer teammates covered Martin and Robert. Philadelphia took the first game, 4-1, and the second, 2-1.

The Sabres, it seemed, would be easy. The Flyers began to celebrate. But the celebration started too soon and almost lost them the Cup. They were tired and many had hangovers when they went out on the ice again. The Sabres downed them two games in a row and tied the series.

Bobby was enraged. His angry tongue lashed out at everyone in sight, including Ed Snider, the Flyers' principal owner. Bobby told Snider that the club management should not have allowed the wild celebration. It wasn't fair to the team or the fans. The Flyers hadn't behaved like champions. People would have the right to think that last year's Cup victory had been a fluke after all.

Snider apologized. He promised that there would be no more celebrating until the Cup was won.

It was a determined Philadelphia team that met the

Sabres in the Spectrum for game No. 5. The Flyers won, 5–1. They came back just as determined for the sixth game. They left the ice with a 2–0 win.

That win gave them the final series and the Stanley Cup for the second year in a row. Now they could celebrate. The Flyers weren't a fluke. They were real champions.

Bobby not only helped to win the Cup but also was again voted the NHL's Most Valuable Player. For the second time in three years, he thus became the recipient of the Hart Trophy. Along with the award, he was given a new Mercedes automobile. The car was a beauty, but it wasn't his style. Before long, he traded it in on a half-ton truck.

The Philadelphia fans, meanwhile, went crazy for their team all over again. The victory celebration was a little more organized this time. There was a parade led by the team. There were marching bands, fireworks, and thousands of fans, all of them cheering, laughing, and singing. Usually, they sang their favorite song: "God Bless America."

Later, a hundred thousand people jammed into John F. Kennedy Stadium to honor the team. Several players gave short speeches. It was Bernie Parent who promised that Philadelphia would take the Cup again when he said to the crowd, "I'll see you all right here again next May 26. Okay?"

It was not to be.

The Flyers made the Cup play-offs easily at the end of the 1975–76 season. They defeated the Toronto Maple Leafs and then the Boston Bruins to reach the finals. Then they came up against the Montreal Canadiens. It was the

Canadiens' year. They had a particularly well-balanced team, with one of the tightest defenses in the league. They romped over the Flyers and took the Stanley Cup in four straight games.

Despite the loss of the Cup, the season was another outstanding one for Bobby Clarke. Once again, sportswriters across North America voted him the Most Valuable Player in the league. The Hart Trophy thus went to Bobby for the third time in his career.

As usual, Bobby's scoring record for the season was impressive. He tallied 30 goals and 89 assists for a total of 119 points. He also passed the 200 mark in goals for his career. And his line—with Bill Barber and Reggie Leach on the wings—became that highest-scoring line in NHL history. In all, the line scored 332 points.

But records and awards aside, one of the highest points of the season for Bobby and the Flyers came when they met the hockey team of the Soviet Army. The Soviet team was on tour of North America. It had beaten some of the NHL's best outfits.

Fans in Canada and the United States were ashamed of the defeats. They looked on the hard-playing Flyers to salvage some of North American hockey's lost honor.

Shero had a plan for the Soviet game. The visitors were known as especially fast skaters. The other NHL teams had worn themselves out trying to keep up with them. To avoid the same problem, Shero set up a defensive line in the middle of the rink. Just one man—the center—was assigned to chase the puck. The plan put a heavy responsibility on Bobby and his fellow centers. But it worked. The Flyers remained fresh and stayed right with the Soviets.

In fact, it worked so well that it infuriated the Soviets. So angry were they that they finally stormed off the ice in protest after Ed Van Imp had floored one of their men with a hard body check.

Spectrum fans and a television audience in the United States and Canada had to wait for sixteen minutes before the visitors returned to the ice. The Soviets came back with little zest for the game. The Flyers outshot them, 49–13, and skated off with a 4–1 victory.

That loss kept the Soviets from going home as the conquering heroes. They had been unable to beat the NHL champions.

Although Bobby had been forced to leave the game in the third period with a deep facial cut, he was particularly happy with the victory. The Soviets had already shown that they were right up there with the best in the world. It's always good to beat the best.

It's even better to be the best.

Today, Bobby's place as one of the best is assured in the world of hockey. He has many good years of play yet ahead of him. He is recognized both as a star player and a team leader. His leadership has made him president of the NHL's Players' Association.

As a star and a leader, he is very concerned about the future of hockey. He wants it to be a game that can be enjoyed by thousands more than the many fans who now enjoy it. But he knows that the violence that had been part of hockey since the NHL was expanded is turning many fans away. He believes the time has come to change things.

In June of 1976, the league, wanting to crack down on

the violence, was talking about passing a new rule. It would call for any player who started a fight on the ice to be thrown out of the game. Bobby, as president of the Players' Association, said that the idea was a good one. But, he added, it didn't go far enough.

He agreed with the players in the Association who wanted to see all those who participated in a fight thrown out, and not just the ones who started it.

Bobby said, "Hockey is good enough on its own that it doesn't need fighting . . . all the brawling hasn't made hockey popular. I know fans in Philadelphia—the best fans in the league now—who have been turned off by the mayhem. . . . I think hockey can be a lot better when you let the talented players perform without fear of getting worked over."

These seemed to be strange words for one of the toughest players on ice to say.

But that's Bobby Clarke for you.

He wants to be the best—but he also wants the best for hockey.

Edward F. Dolan, Jr., and Richard B. Lyttle have been close friends for ten years. Both are native Californians, and each has written several books. The Signal Books mark their first efforts as coauthors.

Mr. Lyttle was raised in Ojai, served in the Navy during World War II, and attended the University of California at Berkeley. He has worked as a cowboy, farmer, newspaper reporter, and editor. He began selling stories and articles for children in the 1950s.

Mr. Dolan's boyhood was spent in Los Angeles. After serving with the 101st Airborne Division during World War II, he attended the University of San Francisco. He began writing when he was in his teens and has also been a teacher and a newspaper reporter.

The two men met while they were reporters for rival newspapers in northern California. Both are avid sportsmen. Mr. Lyttle beats his coauthor regularly at golf. But Mr. Dolan says he can outswim Mr. Lyttle any day of the week.

Mr. Lyttle and his wife, Jean, live in Inverness, a small town next door to the Point Reyes National Seashore north of San Francisco. Mr. Dolan and his wife, Rose, live nearby, in the town of Novato.